Countries of the World

Somalia

by Mike Graf

Consultant:
Dr. Charles Geshekter
Professor of History
California State University, Chico

Bridgestone Books
an imprint of Capstone Press
Mankato, Minnesota

Bridgestone Books are published by Capstone Press
151 Good Counsel Drive, P.O. Box 669, Mankato, Minnesota 56002
http://www.capstone-press.com

Library of Congress Cataloging-in-Publication Data
Graf, Mike.
    Somalia/by Mike Graf.
    p. cm.—(Countries of the world)
    Includes bibliographical references (p. 24) and index.
    Summary: Describes the landscape, culture, food, animals, sports, and holidays
of Somalia.
    ISBN 0-7368-1108-7
    1. Somalia—Juvenile literature. [1. Somalia.] I. Title. II. Countries of the world
(Mankato, Minn.)
DT403.15 .G73 2002
967.73—dc21   2001003231

Editorial Credits
Blake Hoena, editor; Karen Risch, product planning editor; Linda Clavel, designer; Erin Scott,
    SARIN Creative, illustrator; Alta Schaffer, photo researcher

Photo Credits
Audrius Tomonis-www.banknotes.com, 5 (bottom)
Betty Press/Woodfin Camp & Associates, Inc., 8, 10
Cory Langley, cover
Flag Folio, 5 (top)
Jason Laure', 12, 20
Mike Yamashita/Woodfin Camp & Associates, Inc., 6, 18
Photo Researchers/Lew Eatheron, 14; Marcello Bertinetti, 16

1 2 3 4 5 6 07 06 05 04 03 02

Table of Contents

Fast Facts

Name: Somalia
Capital: Mogadishu
Population: About 8 million
Language: Somali
Religion: Islam

Size: 246,199 square miles
(637,657 square kilometers)
*Somalia is slightly smaller than
the U.S. state of Texas.*
Crops: Sugar, bananas, corn, beans

Maps

DJIBOUTI

Gulf of Aden

ETHIOPIA

Somalia

Shabeelle River

Mogadishu

Jubba River

KENYA

*Indian
Ocean*

Somalia

Flag

The Somali flag is blue with a white, five-pointed star. Each point stands for one of Somalia's colonies. Somalia was divided into five colonies. Great Britain ruled two of the colonies. Italy, France, and Ethiopia ruled the other colonies. In the 1960s and 1970s, all the colonies gained their freedom except for the Ethiopian colony. Somalis hope to someday reunite this colony with the rest of Somalia.

Currency

Somalia's unit of currency is the shilling.

In the early 2000s, about 3,700 Somali shillings equaled 1 U.S. dollar. About 2,400 Somali shillings equaled 1 Canadian dollar.

The Land

Somalia is in eastern Africa. Kenya and Ethiopia are west of Somalia. The Gulf of Aden and Djibouti are to Somalia's north. The Indian Ocean is to the southeast. Somalia's coastline is 1,880 miles (3,025 kilometers) long. Somalia has the longest coastline of any African country.

Somalia is mostly flat. The Oogo and Golis mountain ranges are in the north. But the rest of Somalia is dry grasslands, forests, and deserts.

Somalia has two main rivers. The Jubba and Shabeelle Rivers flow through southern Somalia. Most of Somalia's farmland lies between these rivers. Much of Somalia's wildlife also lives in this area.

Somalia has two rainy seasons. They are from April to June and from October to November. During the rainy seasons, there are many short, heavy rains.

Most of Somalia is dry grassland and desert.

Life at Home

Many Somalis have large families. Family groups are called clans. Family members are loyal to their clan and support each other.

At meals, men usually eat first. The women then serve themselves and the children. Men eat separately from the women and children. After dinner, families often gather together around a fire.

Most Somalis live in rural areas. Rural Somalis may be nomadic. They travel from place to place. They search to find food and water for their sheep, goats, and cattle.

Nomadic Somalis build simple huts that can be quickly put up and taken down. These huts are called akals. Somalis tie sticks together to make an akal's frame. They often use animal skins to cover the frame.

About one-third of Somalis live in urban areas. Most Somali cities are along Somalia's east coast. People in cities often fish or have industry jobs.

Nomadic Somalis live in akals.

Going to School

Not all Somali children attend school. In the early 1990s, civil war broke out between the clans in Somalia. Some schools were destroyed. Others have been closed and turned into refugee camps. These camps provide food and shelter for people who have lost their homes because of war.

Somalia does not have many schools operated by the government. Some clans operate local schools. Today, only 1 in 4 Somalis know how to read and write.

In the past, only boys attended school. Today, girls also go to school. Boys and girls often attend separate schools until they go to college.

Somali school children learn reading, writing, math, and languages. They also learn about the Islamic religion.

Most Somali children stop going to school when they are 10 or 11 years old. They then may work on their families' farms.

Today, both girls and boys in Somalia attend school.

Somali Food

A typical Somali breakfast is fried liver with onions and bread. Muufo is a popular type of bread in Somalia. It is flat like pita bread. Somalis eat bread with most meals. Somalis also eat corn porridge in the morning.

Many Somalis buy fresh food at local markets. They buy sorghum, rice, tea, sugar, dates, and vegetables at these markets. Sorghum is a type of grain that people often use to make syrups.

Somalis eat different foods depending on where they live. People who live near rivers may eat crocodile meat. Somalis who live near the coast eat fish. Italy once controlled the southern part of Somalia. Somalis in this area eat a pasta called baasto.

Rural Somalis often raise sheep, goats, and cattle to eat and to sell. Farmers eat cereals, grains, vegetables, and fruits. Nomadic Somalis drink milk and eat fruits and berries.

Somalis buy fruits at outdoor markets.

Clothing

Somalis who live in cities wear modern-style clothing. But they often wear traditional clothing when they are not at work. Rural Somalis mostly wear traditional clothing.

Traditional clothing may include a macaawiis for men. Men wrap this brightly colored cloth around their waist like a skirt. They wear a shirt with a macaawiis. Somali men also wear lengths of white cotton fabric. They wrap the fabric around their bodies like a skirt and a shawl.

Somali women wear long, colorful dresses. They also wear guntiinos. They wrap these pieces of cloth around their bodies. They tie guntiinos at their right shoulder. Married Somali women often wear scarves that cover their head.

Somali women paint their hands and feet with henna dyes. These dyes stain the skin an orange-brown color. Women do this to celebrate a marriage or a birth.

Guntiinos are a traditional type of woman's dress.

Animals

Predators such as lions, cheetahs, and leopards live in Somalia. These animals hunt other animals for food. The leopard is the national symbol of Somalia. It is illegal to hunt leopards.

Somalia has many animals that are typically found in Africa. Elephants, gazelles, antelope, zebras, giraffes, and dik-diks roam Somalia's grasslands. A dik-dik is an antelope that is only 1 foot (.3 meter) tall. Hippopotamuses, pink flamingos, and crocodiles live in Somalia's rivers.

Large termite nests are found on Somalia's grasslands. Termites build nests from their own saliva and waste.

Camels are the most important animals to Somalis. Somalis have written songs and poems about camels. Wealthy families own many camels. Somalis use camels to travel from place to place. They also may eat camel meat to celebrate special religious holidays.

The leopard is the national symbol of Somalia.

Sports and Recreation

Sports are becoming more popular in Somalia. Somalis play soccer and volleyball. They also enjoy boxing and running.

Most Somalis are Muslims. They follow the Islamic faith. Friday is a holy day for Muslims and they do not work. Instead, many Somalis go to the beach on Fridays. At the beach, they swim, walk or jog, and build sand castles. Swimming in the ocean can be dangerous because of sharks. But some beaches in Somalia now have shark-proof nets around them.

Somalis enjoy telling stories. Many of their tales have been told for hundreds of years. Children often gather around older clan members to hear these stories.

Somalis are known for their oral poetry. They often speak their poems during celebrations such as weddings and births.

Somalis often gather to listen to stories or poems.

Holidays and Celebrations

Somalis celebrate many Islamic holidays. One of the most important religious holidays is Ramadan. Somalis fast during the month of Ramadan. They do not eat or drink between dawn and sunset. This act shows faith in their god Allah.

In 1960, the Somali colonies ruled by Great Britain and Italy gained their independence. These colonies then joined together on July 1 to form the Republic of Somalia. Somalis celebrate their independence with parades.

Somalis often dance to celebrate. They dance for three days after a marriage. During the rainy season, boys and girls perform traditional dances to honor the rain.

The Somali year begins at the end of July. At this time, Somalis celebrate the new year with a festival of fire called Neeroosh or Dab-shid. They build bonfires, have water fights, and dance to celebrate this holiday.

Workers take part in an Independence Day parade.

Hands On: Write a Poem

Somalia is considered a nation of poets. Oral poetry is popular in Somalia. Somalis memorize poems and speak them out loud. Children learn Somali history and traditions by listening to poems about historic events. These poems have been passed down from generation to generation.

What You Do

1. Somalis often recite poems about historic or current events. Think of something that recently happened to you. Write a poem about it.
2. Somali poetry uses alliteration instead of rhymes. Each line of a poem has some words that begin with the same consonant or vowel sound. For example, "My **p**arents gave me a **p**uppy."
3. The lines in most Somali poems have an equal number of syllables. For example:
   "My **p**ar-ents gave me a **p**up-py.
   He is **B**ru-tus the Saint **B**er-nard."
   Each line above has eight sound units.
4. Somalis often chant or sing their poems. Poems also may be spoken to music or clapping.
5. Gather an audience to listen to your poem.

Learn to Speak Somali

hello (is it peace?)	ma nabad baa	(MAH na-bad bah)
day	maalin	(MAH-ah-lin)
eat	cun	(OON)
food	cunto	(OON-to)
milk	caano	(AAH-no)
water	biyo	(BEE-yoh)
friend	saaxiib	(SA-ach-eeb)
mother	hooyo	(HOY-oh)
father	aabbe	(AAH-bay)

Words to Know

clan (KLAN)—a group of related families
fast (FAST)—to give up eating for a time
nomadic (noh-MAD-ik)—wandering from place to place
Ramadan (RAHM-i-dahn)—an Islamic religious holiday when Muslims fast
refugee camp (ref-yuh-JEE KAMP)—a place where people who have had to leave their homes can receive shelter, food, and water

Read More

Hassig, Susan M. *Somalia*. Cultures of the World. New York: Marshall Cavendish, 2000.

Schemenauer, Elma. *Somalia*. Faces and Places. Chanhassen, Minn.: Child's World, 2002.

Useful Addresses and Internet Sites

African Studies Center
647 Williams Hall
University of Pennsylvania
Philadelphia, PA 19104-6305

African Studies Program
205 Ingraham Hall
1155 Observatory Drive
University of Wisconsin–Madison
Madison, WI 53706

CIA—World Factbook—Somalia
http://www.cia.gov/cia/publications/factbook/geos/so.html
Somalis—Their History and Culture
http://www.cal.org/rsc/somali/stoc.html

Index